Dare to ask
Maureen Pisani

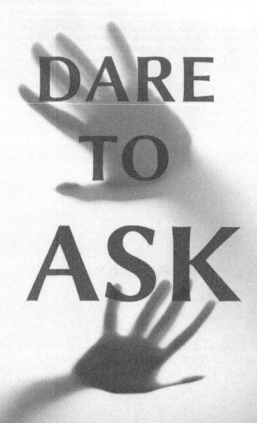

Dare to ask
Maureen Pisani

DARE TO ASK

MY ANSWERS

TO

DEATH,

DYING,

&

WHAT HAPPENS AFTER

By

Maureen Pisani C.Ht., T.N.L.P.

CONTENTS

DEDICATION

This book is dedicated to my Daddy –
Carmelo G. Pisani.

My Dad - a man of honor and integrity. He was the glue of the family and pivotal in my life. He was the best example possible for me in life and death scenarios. He dodged death countless times, and even though he was fully aware of the fact that he was living on borrowed time, he made the most of his life, because he loved at his best.

The teachings I received from my Dad weren't only practical or ethical. I was blessed to learn faith, trust, and unconditional love from him. His death was devastating for me. However, my Dad has continued to love me through space and time. I am reminded almost daily of how much he still loves me. Going through the grieving process opened my eyes and heart to the reality of life without him. I learned firsthand how one goes through the stages of grief. It got me to see how despite his being gone from here, life continued and still does. It was a harsh reality to experience, but a necessary one.

As every day goes by, I find myself more appreciative of the man my Dad was and is. Even though it's been 18 years since he's gone "home," life - although almost normal, will never be. I know I will continue missing his physical presence. Yes, he left that kind of void because he is irreplaceable.

However, my heart and soul know that it's only a matter of time before we are reunited. After all, he's just a breath away.

Dare to ask
Maureen Pisani

ACKNOWLEDGEMENT

Considering that I am tackling such a delicate, sensitive, yet volatile subject, I knew that different perspectives, outlooks, and brains were essential to ensuring that the message shared resonates with as many as possible.

For that reason, I need to acknowledge and thank one of the smartest and most incredible ladies I know – *Patricia McElroy*. She is a genius in her own right, and her extensive knowledge and depth of studies is beyond impressive.

She was kind enough to give me more than a helping hand with this book. Patricia was generous enough to offer me her honest wisdom, critique, advice, and support. I am deeply indebted to her.

It is thanks to your participation, Patricia, that I can achieve my life mission of serving more.
I couldn't have done it without your priceless insight.

Thank you, Patricia, for being who you are – mystical, wise, and authentic in everything you do!

DISCLAIMER

Yes, I am going to discuss several aspects of death, dying, and life after death. Yes, I am utilizing different schools of thought. However, I understand that there are going to be some who disagree with my point of view. That is more than fair. There isn't one topic that will ever get a unanimous agreement, so if someone doesn't agree with my opinion, point of view, or conclusion, it's more than understandable.

I'd like you to ponder this scenario. If I had to go to the depths of the Congo and share with an indigenous tribe that has no concept of cold or snow, that icebergs exist in this world. I would describe icebergs as mountains of solid ice floating in ice-cold water. They wouldn't believe me, fair? Considering the surroundings they're accustomed to, that would also be fair to expect, right? But...would their not believing me negate the existence of icebergs? Of course not!

As you go through segments of this book, if there are aspects where you strongly feel like you're disagreeing with my point of view, all I ask is that you remember the "iceberg scenario." Fair?

I am also aware that some will comment on the fact that I share a lot of "maybe" and "what if" scenarios. I will highlight points and ask for you to be open to the possibilities. What other choice do I have? The only way any of us will have all the answers is after we die. So, considering that I am still a living human being, the best I can offer you is what I think, what I've learned, and what I've witnessed.

Dare to ask
Maureen Pisani

The information here is according to what I know, what I've studied, and what I've experienced. When I share my experiences, please remember that I'm honoring you with my truth. I am sharing this with the intention that my information might soothe some hearts. Personally, I hope that this book will soothe countless hearts and minds.

I will reiterate throughout the book my offer to "take whatever your heart resonates with and discard the rest." After all, I am just a mere mortal, yes, with faith and belief, but just a human.

INTRODUCTION

I am sharing information that I have studied, learned, and collated through the years, experiences that I have lived through and that I know to be true for me. My perspective here is as "Maureen the Hypnotherapist," whose sole mission is to serve millions from the heart.

My goal is to bring peace, understanding, and calmness to a topic that terrifies most – our own mortality and the thought of our loved ones' death. In moments of crisis, when fear runs rampant in our hearts and minds, I would like this book to offer answers to those questions that torment the mind and aggravate the heartbreak.

I will be referencing multiple sources from varying schools of thought. I'm offering it **all** to you, the reader, so you can take what resonates within your heart and discard the rest. YOUR heart will let you know what you feel is true for you.

I AM Catholic. I DO believe in God. I DO believe that Jesus is our Lord and Savior. However, that's just me and my own beliefs. I do appreciate that this world has unlimited religions and beliefs. What I have found to be true is that regardless of what our beliefs are, sometimes, when the unthinkable happens, in the depths of despair, a new piece of information, or a different perspective shared, can soothe our hearts and souls and give us peace.

Truth be told, we have death all around us – in nature. The cycle of life is a constant, whether we acknowledge it or not.

Dare to ask
Maureen Pisani

Whether it's how the plants, vegetables, fruits, or flowers grow, blossom, seed, and die, or whether it's the forever renewing ecosystem in a forest or in the oceans, it's all there. It's just how nature recycles nutrients and energy. And yet, because it's all around us and it's a constant, we tend to gloss over it and ignore its very presence.

There is a huge segment of the adult population that, as children, were raised with a particular religion but then, just because *life happened*, their attendance and participation diminished or discontinued and now they are left with bits and pieces of information that are either incomplete or just incorrect. Whether these children simply participated in the scheduled attendance from obligation or habit, it saddens me that whichever congregation they attended didn't impact them enough for them to keep attending or practicing. I appreciate attending from habit and obligation. I was there once myself, too. [I mention a very definitive moment when all that changed for me in my book Invisible to Invincible.]

As these children grow up, they tend to end up with this hodgepodge of information that only results in hurting them as adults. During a crisis, when they're grieving and searching for something to make a horrible loss make sense, they either realize that they don't have enough information, or the fragments they do remember are incorrect. This just aggravates the situation and intensifies the pain.

My plan is to offer different perspectives. Some of the information shared might be categorized by some as common knowledge, "old wives' tales," "wise women wisdom," or "dogma and doctrine," while others will feel the heaviness in their heart lighten. Some information might also be seen as controversial.

However, I would like to ask you to read the entire book. Give yourself the opportunity to get the whole picture. You're joining me on a journey your heart needs, even though it's a topic your mind has repeatedly pushed away. Please keep in mind that my mission is to serve as many people as I can and to soothe as many hearts as possible.

My message is for those who are overwhelmed with sorrow and need a regular person to share appropriate bits of information that connect the dots in a time and space where nothing makes sense to them.

I will discuss harsh heart-breaking topics because somebody needs to. When you have the unthinkable happen, when children die, when young people die, we are all horrified and heart broken. We have the saying "a parent should never bury a child," but we all know that children do die and yet somehow, we need to make it make sense. We need to know that there is a purpose as to why that happens.

Dare to ask
Maureen Pisani

I am sharing this simply to fill in these blanks. Do your own research. Read the Bible, the Torah, the Koran. Read whichever books your heart is yearning to delve into. Go ask the learned, educated people who have the wisdom, the expertise, and the authority to give you solid answers, please do. I urge you to do so. However, if all you need is that spark of hope, that soothing piece of information, that new perspective for your heart to heal, then this book is for you.

CHAPTER 1

Life is full of interesting ups and downs, beginnings and endings, incidents, and events. We fail, we succeed, we exist, we thrive. Most of us live our lives looking forward to our next chapter. We live hoping that the best is yet to come. However, while we enjoy talking and discussing almost all topics, there is one topic that most of us avoid with every fiber in our being. That topic is our mortality, both our own and that of our loved ones. Most of us are petrified of facing the dying process, death, and what happens after we die.

My intention for this book is to share information from different schools of thought, to fill in the blanks, answer unasked questions, and enlighten and soothe the hearts and minds of many.

Death has been the ultimate of mysteries since the beginning of time. Most cultures have traditions and beliefs regarding death and the afterlife. Some of these traditions like "All Souls Day" and "Dia De Los Muertos" we are familiar with, while other traditions like the Indonesian tradition in Toraja, living with the corpses of their loved ones in their homes [BBC https://youtu.be/knBnQUsj2xo] are way outside our comfort zone.

I remember watching Indira Gandhi's funeral on TV [https://youtu.be/NjsgeaC0qHk], where her son had the *honor* to light up the cremation fire. I remember being torn emotionally.

I understood that this was their culture, but I was also simultaneously horrified at how her own son could set fire to his mother's remains! Different cultures have different religions that go with their traditions.

What I do know is that when a loved one dies, apart from the instant loss we experience, we each go through the grieving process. However, as the days go by, thoughts about what that deceased person experienced, and what he/she is going through, hits us like a ton of bricks. Our human brain ponders unaskable questions regardless of our religious beliefs.

As a therapist, I have had countless sessions helping clients deal with death and grieving. Even though their brain was aware that there is a life-after-death concept, they were still heartbroken because of the *human* questions.

In no way, shape, or form do these questions minimize our religious belief or veracity of our faith, but thoughts – very *human* thoughts - slam our hearts. When my grandmother died on December 4th several decades ago in Malta, an incredibly Catholic country, although very aware of the Catholic doctrine, my aunt commented on how upsetting it was for her that we had had a very wet winter, because her mother always worried about leaks and dampness.

We have thoughts because we are human, and in times of crisis, we drop down to the most human aspect of our being, regardless of how enlightened and awakened we feel we are.

CHAPTER 2

I like putting the cards on the table, so to speak. I like starting something on a solid foundation. For that reason, I'm going to tackle what most seem to skip over, the most fundamental of truths. In my opinion, we, as human beings, cannot and will not *ever* fully understand God. We are simply too limited to comprehend His immensity.

As the eternal student, I have delved into many worlds, exploring and discovering fascinating information that simply makes this world even more beautiful to me. One of the more awe-inspiring was the study of the human body. The intricacies and nuances of the human body's anatomy and function, for me, are solid proof that God exists. None of us has the capability, wherewithal, or foresight to design an organism so complex, delicate, and yet so incredibly resilient.

I am in awe as to how amazing the human brain is, yet up until now, from what scientists have discovered, there are still undiscovered aspects of the brain's capabilities. The concept of Neuroplasticity is opening new worlds to us, with more understanding as to how the brain functions. However, scientists are more than aware that they haven't discovered or understood everything about the brain. This is why I share my opinion about the brain, because it's a known fact that the brain is the ultimate frontier, one that still hasn't yet been explored or understood completely.

As the neuroscience world continues breaking barriers, all we know is that the more they discover, the more the scientists are aware of how much more there is yet to explore. The human brain is an incredible masterpiece. It **is** phenomenal. However, even with all its magnificence, the human brain and its currently known capabilities notwithstanding, **is** limited. Why, you ask? Simply because it is a *human* brain!

We know through science that the colors ultraviolet and infrared exist in the spectrum of light, but our eyes don't **see** them. The eyes and the brain are incapable of receiving and recognizing those frequencies. We also know that dog whistles work from the response of dogs around us, but our ears don't register the sound, because our ears and our brain are incapable of picking up and recognizing those frequencies, too.

Please keep in mind, I am just delineating where the line in the sand is for all of us. We can perceive & acknowledge so much of the world around us, but we don't perceive everything.

When it comes to our beliefs, cultures have been aware of a higher power since the beginning of time. Throughout history, there is evidence over the eons of time that man created deities and worshiped several gods in one way or another. Some had multitudes of deities, like the Egyptian and Greek cultures, while other cultures like the Jewish religion had one God. In an attempt to understand how these deities worked, mankind gave them human attributes.

Because we are who we are – humans - we did the best with what we had. We utilized our thinking and imagination and created a narrative according to what we can connect with and comprehend. What humans have done over the millennia is to attempt to explain God's immensity through personification.

The definition of personification is the attribution of a personal nature or human characteristics to something nonhuman, or the representation of an abstract quality in human form.

It wasn't done maliciously. On the contrary, it was done in an effort to make God relatable.

We have all been told and taught that God is this *wise old man with a flowing white beard* sitting on a throne up in Heaven. I totally get that for mankind to have some sort of relationship, awareness, or simple recognition, we had to describe Him in human terms, but man didn't just stop there.

I appreciate how lofty of a project it had to have been, when eons ago, men found themselves in situations where they had to describe who their God was. Just think of Abraham, attempting to explain why he was leaving the land of Ur. How could he possibly explain God? I also appreciate that if Moses attempted to be metaphysical with the Pharaoh, it would have backfired on him horribly.

What I would like to point out is that all we need to accept is the basic bottom line: God is more than we can ever understand.

However, to be fair to all those questioning this point, I'd like to add this perspective. Considering that we're told that God created us in His image, who's to say if portions of the brain's capabilities that are still yet to be discovered can perceive everything else? After all, considering that we are God's creations, and He can do anything, He could have made us capable, couldn't He? There definitely is the possibility, but alas, science is not there yet. So, even though the brain as a human organ is limited, the brain as God's creation has not been 100% explained yet. Fair?

So, coming from a very grounded human standpoint, I humbly think that we, in our best-case scenarios, can be beyond grateful that He has seen fit to bless us with everything we are.

A few years ago, a priest shared with me the best explanation to delineate what our brains can conceive and what they cannot. Imagine horses in a beautiful stable, watching their master walk up the hill to the mansion. One horse says to the other, "I bet you he has the largest stalls with the freshest hay in there." As you can see, that's all the horses' point of reference would be, right? Stalls and hay. So, as they were conjuring up what the best possible scenario for them was, they came up with "large stalls and freshest hay" as the epitome of luxury. That's exactly what mankind has done for millennia when it comes to describing and explaining God, his capabilities, and Heaven.

To make things even more interesting, we didn't just stop there. No, we continued "humanizing" God to the point where we determined what He can or cannot do!

Dare to ask
Maureen Pisani

We have determined which religion is right and which religion is wrong, which belief is correct, and which one is erroneous.

The Island of Malta was one of the first countries to become Catholic, when St. Paul was shipwrecked there in 60AD. The island is mentioned in the Acts of the Apostles by name. Growing up on the island of Malta included experiencing religion in a way that was more than just words for me. It was in our culture, in our vernacular, in our daily life, and in our schedules. Especially in my family, faith and belief were part and parcel of our existence. I cherish those years.

One of the things I learned during that time, was the concept of the "Anonymous Christian." [In the Jesuit theology it's called the "non-conscious Christian".] It was explained to me like this: if there's a person living in an indigenous village in the middle of the Amazonian jungle, where the word of God hadn't arrived yet, but this person is *with intention* choosing right from wrong and living in integrity (instead of cheating others), that person, although not officially converted to the official and traditional description of what we consider a Catholic religion, would be considered a Christian because that person is living his/her life in a "Christ-like" manner.

You might know that the Judeo-Christian religions started with Abraham in Ur, in the Middle East. As the story goes, the protagonists and the chosen people travelled west all the way to Judea, Bethlehem, and Nazareth, and then flourished through and around the Mediterranean, eventually having the conversion efforts expand east and north through Europe.

What about the people in Asia, Indonesia, Australia, and the Americas, before the Conquistadors colonized the Americas and the rest of the world? Did God forget about those people? No, of course not. The Aztecs, Incas, Buddhists, Hindus, and all the indigenous peoples had their religions, their beliefs, and their traditions. So, were their religions wrong, bad, or sacrilegious?

Think about it for a moment. We have a lot of "leaders" who stand on their soap box and preach THE word while condemning other beliefs. However, what if they all lead to God?

Humor me for a second and imagine a massive tree with branches that go in every direction, where each branch has thousands of leaves. If I were a leaf facing west, wouldn't that be the view that I can, in full honesty, claim to be the best view in life? But what about a leaf that's facing east, north, or south? Couldn't they also claim the same? Would they be wrong? Wouldn't all of us be right, despite having a different view?

So, what IF (remember we're only using our human brain to explore this) the world was the tree, and the branches were the different peoples, different religions, and different ideologies, and God was the tree trunk? Wouldn't that make God true for each and every one of us? And if we believe that God is Eternal Unconditional Love, wouldn't He love us exactly for who we are in spite of our religion? Because truth be told, He had us be born in that particular segment of the world from the get-go. And regardless of our religion, wouldn't be we judged according to our acts, deeds, and intentions?

I need to make something clear here. I am assuming that each of us is living our every day with full intention to choose right over wrong.

This is how the definition of sin was explained to me. Each of us finds ourselves having to make a decision between choice "A" and choice "B." If we're not sure about the consequences, and we make a choice utilizing all the information we have at the time, and that choice is made from a loving perspective, even if our choice was incorrect, it's just chalked up as a mistake.

However, if we know that choice "A" has negative consequences that will hurt people and we choose choice "A" with intention, then and only then, because of the willful awareness of choosing to hurt others, will that choice, that action, be considered a sin.

There is also something else we need to keep in mind. Something that is just between you and God and is what morality, karma, and ultimate judgment revolve around – INTENTION.

You see, the same action can be either a good or a bad deed, according to one's intention. No one other than you and God know what your internal intention is, but your true intention is what's tipping the balance between the deed being good or bad.

Let me explain. Let's say I'm walking with my friend Jane, and she accidentally trips and is falling to the ground. In that instant, as soon as I realize Jane might get hurt, I reach out to grab and save her from splattering her face on the ground. If internally, I reach out to help her for the simple fact that I want to help Jane and prevent severe injury, then that's a good deed. If, however, I think to myself, "let me grab and save Jane from falling to show everyone around us how incredibly strong I am," then that's coming from Ego, which makes it a bad deed. See the difference?

So, intention, this secret aspect of us, of our soul, is essential to the outcome of how we live our life. Remember, that God is omniscient – all knowing, so of course He knows each and every one of our deeds and knows what intention backed each thought, choice, decision and deed.

CHAPTER 3

Truth be told, I am yearning to die. No, I do not have suicidal tendencies, but whenever you hear that "Maureen died," please immediately realize that I am finally genuinely happy. Yes, I appreciate that this is a strange philosophy to adopt, but as I walk you through how I've come to this bewildering conclusion, I'm hoping that you end up not only understanding my explanation but agreeing with me.

Death. What is death? I appreciate that it's a strange question to ask, but if I asked a few people of different religions, different traditions, different cultures, I'd probably receive a few different responses. Fair?

I have to admit that I've pondered this topic a lot, and I think there's a misnomer that we've all mistakenly accepted. We all talk about life and death. We think of life as the time between birth and death, correct? But why are we calling that time "life" when we're alive in utero and we're alive after death? Wouldn't it be better if we titled our time here in the body as our "earthly existence?"

When I think of that part of me that's alive, I know it's my soul. It has been alive since the beginning of time, and will continue to be alive through eternity. To experience this life, our soul connected with a physical body so it can experience each and every moment through our central and autonomic nervous systems, which will then reach and affect the brain. As we experience it all, our mind and our consciousness, which in actuality is our soul, is evolving and raising its vibrations with each lesson accrued.

Dare to ask
Maureen Pisani

As you can see, I consider the experience of death simply as a transition, during which our soul releases this carbon-based biodegradable shell we call a body and enters higher realms. Most of us call these higher realms heaven or nirvana.

Heaven. What exactly *is* heaven? From my Catholic teachings, I know that God, the Holy Trinity, the Virgin Mary, all the saints, angels, and all the good people are there, right? We know that God is Eternal Unconditional Love, so it has to be a good place, right?

As the saying goes – we all wish to go to heaven, but nobody wants to die. However, if you ask most people, they're terrified of dying! When you ask them specifics, the basis for all their fears is "the fear of the unknown."

Here's my take on heaven. Here's how I personally see it. Again, take what resonates in your heart from this and discard the rest. However, please read the entire explanation. How is one to come to an educated decision if one doesn't read the whole thing?

I would like you to imagine that a parent tells his/her children that they just bought tickets to Disney World! Not just the basic entrance tickets, but the super-deluxe VIP tickets. Can you imagine how excited and happy those children are going to be? Those children's days are happier because they know that *at some point,* they are going to Disney World! They have no idea **when,** but simply because their parent said that they bought the tickets, the children are happier.

Now, I would like you to imagine a similar scenario where the parent tells his/her children that they just bought super-deluxe VIP tickets to Disney World *and* they are going in June! It doesn't matter if there's another 11 months, 6 months or a couple of months to wait, because the children have a date, and the closer the date gets, the happier, the more enthusiastic, and the more excited the children will be. Fair?

Between you and me, I know for a fact that heaven is better than Disney World. I know that however my mind can conceive heaven is a drop in the bucket from what God's Immensity has created so that Jesus, our Lord and Savior, can describe it to the penitent thief as "paradise." [Luke 23:39-43 Catholic Edition (RSV-2CE)]

Personally, I'd love to die today because that would mean that I'll get to enjoy God and His Eternal Unconditional Love from today. So, when my time comes, please keep in mind, I finally made it to paradise. The intensity and purity of love I will be surrounded by is simply impossible for me to understand while I still walk this earth. However, I can appreciate that it will be tremendous!

There are people whom I titled the *lucky ones*, people who have been through an incredible experience who can give us some insight. These are the people who have had near death experiences. There are several who have technically, medically died, left their body, went toward that white light, and because it wasn't their time yet, returned to their body and to their existence here on Earth. Only they returned transformed.

Each and every person I've encountered who has had a Near Death Experience (N.D.E.) comes back peaceful, full of love, sharing how amazing the other side is.

They share how peaceful, how loving, how welcoming the other side is. They have a demeanor about them that is so peaceful and easy going. That glimpse that they got soothed their soul so much that now nothing's stressful, nothing's a big deal, and everything is easier to handle and seen in its proper perspective. Everything they go through is juxta-positioned against that one monumental & transformative experience. Compared to what they witnessed and felt, everything here on earth is so miniscule, it's nothing to worry about. I've noticed an incredible knowing within these individuals. Some call the source God, some the Universe, some simply Pure Love, but all agree it's an inexplicable intensity of peace, acceptance, safety, and love.

They share how incredible everything was, but repeatedly state that they don't have the right words to describe it all properly. They share that everything they perceived was through thought. They experienced things that they easily describe as beautiful, amazing, and beyond loving, but again reiterate that human words do not do it justice. Yes, it was just that awe-inspiring.

CHAPTER 4

Let's talk about love. I would like to start with a common foundation. We can ponder a mother's love as a standard of true, supportive, doting love for her child. Yes, I am assuming that this is a truly balanced and pure love from mother to child. When we consider the best-case scenario here, we can appreciate that the mother's maternal instinct is caring, vigilant, attentive, and ever-present. She prioritizes her child and caters to it in a way so that baby needs for nothing. Therefore, when that foundation is set, that baby grows up in a positive, supportive, and loving environment that allows for physical, mental, emotional, and spiritual growth to occur in a healthy and harmonious way.

[I am of course aware that some babies grow up without a mother, or a scenario when love is conditional, or their mother was a source of pain. I only utilized the mother's love as a basis where most of us can conceive the optimum setting.]

Now, let's talk about another love we can easily connect with – romantic love - all the stages of romantic love. In the beginning of a relationship, romantic love is exciting, endearing and makes us feel so much! We feel chosen, cherished, pampered, special, thought of, cared for, and so much more. As the relationship progresses and the bond between two people strengthens, that romantic love transforms into a committed love, where the partners feel secure, supported, and safe in their commitment to each other. They **know** that whatever happens, their partner **will** be by their side. They **know** they can depend on the other person to help them through every single situation in their life.

They know that the other half of the couple is trustworthy, loyal, and in integrity. They understand that life has ups and downs, but they are okay with all the chapters they face, because they know in the depths of their being that they will face each chapter **together!** For the lucky ones who have this experience, cherish it! It's an incredible blessing!

So, as we think of all the aspects of love – true love, in all of its variations, you can see how these two examples are just that - examples of all the varying intensities and kinds of love we tend to experience, receive, and give. What about the love shared between best friends? What about that bond between people known as "brotherly love," that is so strong and honorable that it lasts a lifetime? All this love, and yet, we are just human!

How much more intense, more pure, more accepting, more forgiving, more compassionate, and more "_____" (fill in the blank) is God's love? Yes, I give you the choice to fill in your own qualities, because each of us has different qualities we'd love to experience.

Keep in mind, that as much as the mom loves her child, there are still going to be occasions where the kid is beyond naughty and the mother loses her temper. As much as the couple love each other, there is still going to be the occasion when a breakdown in communication occurs and the partners argue, but love continues on.

God's love is eternal and unconditional. He is always there ready to forgive us, to welcome us back home, ready to soothe our very essence. AND God gifts us all this love for the rest of eternity! Again, I urge you to think about the words we've been given, words we have become accustomed to. Eternity – pause and think about it for a second. Eternity, never ending time. Again, we have no concept of it because everything we do here on earth is time-based.

So, IF you can imagine the happiest moment of your life, where in your mind, body, heart, and soul everything is at its best, how phenomenal would it be to have that state of existence for a thousand years, or a million years, or 888 million years, keep going…. Eternity is longer! It's for the rest of time! Even though your mind can ponder it, please keep in mind that heaven is even better than all that and for an even longer expanse of time.

I know that some have a "celebration of life" instead of a funeral. Even though we miss the loved one who just died, we truly should be celebrating when a loved one dies, because that simply means that this person whom we loved dearly, he/she is now enjoying bliss – true, eternal, unconditional love, and peace for the rest of time. And... isn't that what we all hope we receive?

CHAPTER 5

I appreciate that I've mentioned "eternity" and the "rest of time" several times, but I know that some of you are asking how reincarnation comes into play here.

I will start my explanation with a question. Do you believe that God is omnipotent? *The official definition of "omnipotent" is having unlimited power, able to do anything.* Well, if you do, you have to acknowledge, just like I do, that that means that He can do anything, right? And, if God can do *any*thing, doesn't that mean that He can do *every*thing? God is also omniscient, meaning He is all knowing.

Allow me to share some foundational information so we can build this together. Fair? Good.

In the Judeo-Christian religions, we know that at the moment of conception, as soon as the ovum is fertilized, a human life begins. As soon as that happens, everything is set – date of birth, family of origin, all the experiences that person is meant to live through, including the date of death. Everything is predetermined, everything is written, and God's plan for that individual starts unfolding. In this scenario, we have one soul, one human body, one life to live and at the end of it we (hopefully) go to heaven.

In the Reincarnation ideology, the theory is that each of us starts out as a free unlimited spirit. Once we are ready for another incarnation (another human life), we set up a contract that has our date of birth, our family of origin, and all the lessons and experiences we choose for that life, including the date of our death. In this scenario, we have one soul with many lives and many human bodies. The purpose of multiple lives is believed to be because the soul needs to accrue a complete set of experiences and lessons. Each of these experiences raises the soul's vibration, and only once all the lessons and experiences have been completed and the soul's vibration has been raised to the appropriate level, will that soul enter nirvana. In my humble opinion, I think that heaven and nirvana are the same space.

When I share that the soul needs to accrue all experiences to raise the vibration high enough to enter nirvana, I do have to share that it means *every* kind of experience – even the most horrific of sorts. This includes situations like a loved one being murdered, dying through suicide, or going through an unforeseen tragedy. As shocking and as heartbreaking as these events are, the soul needs to accrue every experience so that it will never have to go through it again. There are no words to make this topic lighter, but please keep in mind that the entire set means exactly that - the good, the bad, and the ugly. For those of you who have been in any of these scenarios, my heart breaks for you, but please keep in mind that your loved one's soul will never have to go through that again.

Please keep in mind that when someone we know goes "home" at an early age, that means we also chose to go through the experience of losing someone young. Basically, many souls complete several life lessons through one horrific experience.

I appreciate that sometimes life is beyond harsh. When we face these unthinkable tragedies, offering these perspectives to the mourning family and friends can ease the pain.

Remember, the analogy of the leaves on opposite sides of the tree that I mentioned before? Well, considering that I was born on the Island of Malta, an intensely Catholic Island, I grew up with my set of beliefs. The question is, what would I have grown up with if I had been born in India? I know that I'm asking controversial questions, but all I need you to do is to think about it. Open up to the possibilities. Allowing the "maybe" or the "what if" scenarios to float in your mind will allow you to receive new information that will soothe your heart and mind.

Knowing that God is omnipotent, doesn't that mean that **both** scenarios can be simultaneously correct? Who are we to say what He can or cannot do? All I'm asking you to do is ponder the possibilities.

I'm not telling you to believe one version or the other. All I'm asking you to do is to think about the possibilities. If you read any books on reincarnation, especially where young children are involved, the evidence is so incredibly overwhelming that it's beyond disconcerting.

Yes, I am choosing "disconcerting" with intention, because as a Catholic, a religion where the concept of reincarnation is rejected, the evidence available simply makes one's mind wonder. Even if I allowed for a percentage of people recounting their experiences to be lying, I know that not all of them were misrepresenting the truth. Some simply *had* to be telling the truth. Reading the testimonials of 6-year-olds, having personal, private, secret code names that plane crews or cloistered nuns utilized only within their special groups, leaves one, admittedly, at least befuddled.

When I read books about reincarnation, even though I am a Catholic with a strong faith, I had to admit to myself that I couldn't shut the door on reincarnation and dismiss it completely. This realization shook me to my core. However, that's when the "God is omnipotent" realization came to me. In *my* world, I *know* that God truly can do everything.

So, again, I ask you to think about it and just let your heart and soul receive it. For us humans to say "this" is acceptable and "that" is unacceptable is tantamount to saying, "God can do this" but "God cannot do that." And that, my friends, is utterly preposterous!

Now's the time to discuss "eternity" and "time." We know that "time" is a human concept. Therefore, we have to pause and assess what "eternity" means now. When we talk about reincarnation, the process where the same soul returns for another human life, we are told that the interval between lives isn't a predetermined, pre-set amount of time.

What if both exist? What if both exist simultaneously? Remember that statement – "God is omnipotent"? The second your human brain says, "NO. They can't exist simultaneously," you have taken a very harsh stance opposing God! Who are you to say God cannot do something? I appreciate that this question ruffles your feathers, and I do apologize, but I do have to ask it.

I know because I was there. I went through that thinking pattern. Everything we stand on comes from human thinking. Everything we utilize as arguing points, whether faith-based or science-based, is all human-based.

Here's something that's still baffling the best of human brains. In the world of Quantum Physics, scientists have discovered that the smallest unit of mass is actually vibrating energy that sometimes behaves like particles, and at other times behaves like waves. The lower the level of vibration, the more solid the properties; while the higher the vibration, the more liquid or gaseous the properties.

They have also observed these vibrating energies, so they know that *sometimes* the energy is there, visible to the observer, and *sometimes* it isn't! No one knows where the energy goes when it isn't present! Yes, this **is** scientific fact. Now that you have this piece of information, what if when the vibrating energy is not present, it's gone to an alternate universe, or a parallel universe, or a different time?

What if we are all currently living multiple lives simultaneously and just can't realize it due to our human brains' limited capabilities? What if our brains are wired to only perceive the reality we are living in, even though we're living in multiple dimensions simultaneously? What if God made it so, so we just don't go crazy due to the overload?

We cannot realize it, but the bottom line I am highlighting here is that God CAN. God in all his immensity can conceive it, create it, and make it happen…. BECAUSE HE IS GOD. That, my friends, is what I consider true, blind faith. I KNOW HE CAN for the simple reason that HE IS GOD, THE MOST HIGH.

CHAPTER 6

Why is this important to share? Because when we face the unthinkable, the death of a child, the death of the one person we loved the most, or go through an unexpected tragedy, we struggle with it, because we need it to make sense somehow. However, when we are in the throes of horrible emotional pain, we cannot think straight, and spinning our wheels only aggravates the wound and intensifies the loss.

The reason I've shared so much with you is because I need you to have the foundation and scaffolding over which to build the next layer.

As I mentioned before, the date of birth, all the life experiences, and the date of death are all predetermined, regardless of which school of thought you subscribe to. So that means, that the second life begins, the clock is ticking.

The good news is that **never** will any one of us die a moment before we are meant to die, which instantaneously means that each death you have had to face and mourn was meant to be. I am sorry. I know this is a hard fact to absorb, but I know it to be true. There are several quotes in the bible about how our days are counted, like in Psalms, "your (God's) eyes saw my unformed body; all the days ordained for me were written in your book before one of them came to be." Psalm139:15 [Catholic Edition (RSV-2CE)]

I would like to offer you an analogy as an explanation. I would like you to think about baking a cake. You have all the ingredients, and you mix them up appropriately, which leads you to having a batter. Then you pour the batter into a pan and place that pan in the oven for a certain amount of time. You then, with intention, put a timer on so you can take the pan out when the cake is ready. Fair? And... only when the timer goes off do you (i) know that the cake is done and (ii) do you take the pan out of the oven.

What if you can see how close to life this analogy truly is?

When in utero, the physical body is literally being formed, so we can see how the batter emerges as a human being after 9 months inside. However, during our time on earth, the time we call our life, there are other aspects of ourselves that are "baking" – our mental, emotional, and spiritual "selves" are experiencing every moment, to learn from it, to accrue the lesson, to upgrade our perspective, to grow from that experience on a mental and emotional level, and to raise our soul's vibration.

We have all the right ingredients, but we're not ready yet. What we consider "life" is our time getting ready. When our timer dings, we are then "removed" from the environment which was assisting us in getting ready!

Because, truth be told, the batter is only identified as a cake once it's completely baked, right? So, what if we could acknowledge that here, on Earth, while we're going through this process called "life," we are not the best version of ourselves yet? What if we can acknowledge that only when we leave this "valley of tears" and enter heaven will we be at our best? Will we truly be living? What if we can just see that as a possibility?

I can share two personal experiences. My sister, Brigitte, was born completely normal. She was a healthy baby in all ways. She was given a penicillin shot as a preventive measure when she was 3 days old and died within 3 hours of receiving that injection. As one can expect, it was beyond tragic. Yes, a horrifying experience, one that didn't make sense to everyone who was affected by it.

On the other hand, then, I also witnessed this. My Dad had three heart attacks in one week when he was 50 years of age. He was given four weeks to live. He was in a medical coma for 60 days, after which my Dad woke up simply due to the grace of God. There was no medical reason why he survived. He lived for an additional 25 years, suffering around 16 more heart attacks and undergoing a quintuple cardiac bypass. After all that, he died of a pulmonary embolism at 75.

See what I mean? My Dad technically, medically, should have died when he was 50, and technically when he had the next and the next and the next heart attack! But he didn't. Dad only died when it was according to God's plan, just like Brigitte did.

Each of us comes with a mission to complete. Some of us take 80 or so years to complete it, while others take a shorter time. Sometimes, the mission is a lesson for only our soul, while sometimes, the mission is being the cause or the catalyst for the resultant transformation stemming from the individual's demise.

When children die, it's beyond heart-breaking, but even in the depths of despair and loss, please keep this in mind: that child is now free of the human limitations and restraints and is enjoying God's Eternal and Unconditional Love.

When young people die, we usually hear that lamentation, "they were taken way before their time." As you can see now, that is an incorrect sentence. When young people die, they died because it *was* their time. I totally appreciate and agree that it's the worst scenario possible from a human standpoint. Yes, I agree that a parent should never have to bury a child, but if it is meant to happen, there is nothing we can do about it. The best approach, when the time is right, is to share that this young person is now receiving God's love. As heartbroken as the parents might be, even in the depths of their tragedy, their hearts will hold onto *that* piece of knowledge.

There is something else I would like to highlight. In the reincarnation ideology, an individual determines which experiences they will go through before the incarnation. So, when young people die, it was something that that soul had chosen to go through.

That young person's soul deemed it necessary to live that experience in order to accrue that lesson and raise their vibration one more notch. The interesting part is that every member of that young person's life also had it in their soul's mission to experience the death of a young family member, so their soul's vibration could also be raised.

How different an energy is it when one realizes that one death helped so many of the youngster's loved ones. All of them, now having gone through it in this lifetime, will never have to experience that kind of loss ever again.

CHAPTER 7

Regardless of how the death occurs, we "survivors" feel the loss.

I can share with you that my Dad died in less than a minute. He was living a normal life, fully coherent, fully functioning and enjoying his day, when he suddenly felt dizzy, sat down, took a breath, and died. Yes, literally that fast. For those present, it was beyond shocking. To share that piece of information seems incomprehensible. One of my cousins, who was in the room when Dad passed away described my Dad's death like someone just "switched him off." One second, he was there, the next – gone.

Then, there is the opposite situation, where the person has been sick for a while, and the disease has progressed to the point where that person has been placed in hospice. Even though, in some cases hospice has been known to last up to several months, professionals prepare the family that once in hospice, things usually happen relatively quickly, meaning that the individual is expected to die in the near future. However, there are situations where that does not happen, and the patient is either extremely sick or drops into a coma and hangs on. The family members are torn, emotionally speaking. There's a part of them that is holding onto every extra moment they have with their loved one, but there's another part of them that hates witnessing their loved one suffer. The question in everyone's mind is "why is it taking so long?"

The reason this happens is when that person's soul is going through a cleansing while still on this earthly plane. According to my Catholic beliefs, I understand that after death, souls go to purgatory to be cleansed. We are also told that this process is intense. That's why we have masses offered for the souls of our loved ones, to ease their cleansing and help them get to heaven faster.

In actuality, it's been explained to me that it might be less intense if your loved one goes through an earthly cleansing instead of a cleansing in purgatory. Plus, as the family hovers around the dying loved one, if it comes to the point where the patient is unconscious and the family members are still vigilant, caring, and loving, then every action that the family members implement is considered a good deed, a credit for their own soul. Positive karma, if you will.

Karma is a Sanskrit term that literally means "action" or "doing." In the Buddhist tradition, karma refers to actions driven by intention which lead to future consequences. Those intentions are considered to be the determining factor in the kind of rebirth in samsara, the cycle of rebirth.

In different cultures, we know this concept as "what goes around, comes around."

[Personally, especially when working with children or advising parents who are dealing with unruly children, I always share this perspective. One of the best things to teach young people (even as young as 3), is that a good deed leads to a reward, while a bad deed leads to a consequence.

Most adults live by this rule. It would help everyone around to have this perspective in their lives from as young of an age as possible. This rule teaches accountability that helps us all be better human beings. It helps us be more ethical, more responsible, and more understanding at the very least.]

What about people who either do not have a strong belief, people who aren't quite sure, or people who choose to be atheists? What happens to them?

In the beginning of the book, I mentioned being frank and bringing up different perspectives that might be controversial. This is one of those. Again, I ask you to just keep an open mind.

I, personally, believe that God exists. I believe that in spite and despite an individual's belief or strength of faith, God loves each and every one of us more than we can ever understand. Personally, I think God will receive each and every one of us with open arms, welcoming us "home."

For the atheists, here's my question to them – You're living life asserting that there is no God, right? What are you going to do when you come face to face with Him? Atheists' responses have been – "Well, that's your opinion." That's absolutely true, it is.

Here's something I've offered atheists in session. What if one lived life thinking God existed, only to die and find out that there wasn't a God. What would one do then? However, what if one lived life thinking God didn't exist, only to die and find out that God does exist. What would one do *then*? So I ask on which bet are you willing to gamble your soul?

Because we were gifted with free will, we do get to choose. However, I would like to offer the atheists an opportunity to think things through before giving their final answer.

Again, my role here is to get one thinking. Regretting one's decision after one dies, when it's all said and done, is wasted energy. At that point, there's nothing you can do to rectify the situation. Once we reach that point, there are no do-overs!

With this book, I'm hoping to get people curious enough to take a deeper dive into what they truly know and believe. Having a deeper understanding and a stronger connection to God tends to help us through the valleys of life. If there's even an iota of curiosity within you, honor it. Do your due diligence. Your soul deserves at least that much, don't you think?

CHAPTER 8

Life – what exactly is it?

The bible describes Adam's creation as "And the Lord God formed man of the slime of the earth, and breathed into his face the breath of life, and man became a living soul." Genesis 2:7 [Catholic Edition (RSV-2CE)]. Personally, I think of our soul as God's Breath within us. I know that the soul is a living entity. It always has been, it is, and it will always be - alive.

In Traditional Chinese Medicine (T.C.M.), the life force energy is called "qi" (chi). T.C.M., this incredible school of knowledge, appreciates the effect qi has on the physical body. Overall health, how I understand it, is the harmony achieved between the yin and yang of qi. For some, yin is noted to be more subdued while the yang is known to be more of a forceful energy. Yin is usually expressed as the feminine, while yang is the masculine.

In health, if an organ has yang attributes, then it is said to have too much qi in it. Some call it a build-up or stagnation of energy. Other times, if an organ displays yin attributes, then it is known to have a deficiency of qi. For health to triumph, there needs to be continuous ebbs and flows of qi within each cell for each organ and for each system to function in a synergistic and harmonious manner.

If you have ever seen a loved one in his/her casket, then you've noticed that even though you recognize that person, you are also incredibly aware that there is something very different about them. I appreciate that the person is dead, but what I'm talking about is something else. The absence of qi, the absence of God's breath from within the body, instantly transforms that person from our loved one to a biodegradable carbon-based shell.

There have been studies [1907 publication from Dr. D. MacDougall, Massachusetts] where bodies where weighed before and after death. The corpses were found to be consistently 21 grams lighter than when the bodies were alive. Dr. Duncan MacDougall postulated that the soul weighed that mysterious 21grams.

We know that the First Law of Thermodynamics states that "Energy cannot be created nor destroyed." So, just as we know that the body, through decomposition, breaks down and repurposes this biodegradable shell we call a body, something must happen to the soul too. Right?

That gets one to start asking some pretty serious questions like: What is the soul? How do we connect with our soul? How does one identify which part of me, which part of you, is the soul? In my opinion, your soul is your essence, the part of you that will always live. Your soul is your knowing, your consciousness. There's something you can do to explore and discover that part of you that is your soul.

I practice this exercise to connect with my consciousness. I like to do this before falling asleep, but you might prefer to choose a different time. Choose a color that represents your life essence. Then imagine you're completely filled with that color inside. I lay in bed and imagine vacuuming up my life essence from the tips of my toes upwards, through my legs, into my abdomen, from the tips of my fingers through my arms, into my chest, from my torso through my neck and throat, until all of my life essence is in my brain.

With practice you will learn to disconnect from the body, where you can imagine being just a thought. When you're only in your brain and you can connect with only thinking… that portion of you…the portion that is still alive and thinking is your consciousness, your soul. At least, that's how I see it. There's a purpose to do this exercise.

I would like you to think about this with me. Take a moment and ask, "Who am I?" Go past the male/female/young/old/thin/fat/blonde/brunette labels and ask yourself again. "Who am I?" Take it seriously. It's incredibly cathartic, effective, and it will allow you to truly connect with your life's mission.

Close your eyes and ask again "Who am I?" "What's my soul's mission?" "Why am I alive?" Release all the labels, the expectations, the frivolities of earthly achievements, and the fluff of materialism, and bring it down to what's true and real – your soul. Your life's mission. Why are YOU alive right now? Ask yourself, "Why am I alive right now?"

Dare to ask
Maureen Pisani

Give yourself some time. Allow what needs to present itself to show up in your awareness. You can repeat this exercise as often as you'd like. You can do it periodically, to see if there are any changes or upgrades since your last practice run. It will help you connect with your life's purpose. Having awareness of your life's purpose is probably the most important thing for us to live a truly impactful life, a life with direction.

Once you're done with your exercise, remember to allow all your life essence to flow back down through your entire body, all the way back down to every cell.

Here are my answers – I, Maureen, am alive right now because I still have a mission to complete. My mission is to serve as many as I can in the best way I can. I take it upon myself to live every moment (as is humanly possible) with full awareness and intention. I strive to choose right from wrong with every decision, while being fully aware that sometimes the very humanity of my nature will fail me, and I will choose foolishly. I am here to serve, guide, and teach, by word, deed, and example. I am here to learn, to live through all the chapters of life and accept that each chapter has a purpose, a lesson my soul needs. I am here to experience the easy and the difficult. I am here to be a witness of God's immensity. I am here to open peoples' eyes and hearts. I am here to bring hope, light, faith, understanding and love to all who accept me. I am here to love and be loved.

I am here to realize my humanity and all its limitations, and to acknowledge that sometimes even when I do my utmost and my best, I will not succeed. I will fail. I will be rejected. I will be betrayed. I will be abandoned. I will lose what means the most to me, because in every scenario, there's a lesson in it for me to better my soul. God's plan for me will always triumph. God's plan is to teach me and my soul how to serve at our best and those skills come from experiencing every aspect of life.

I am here for as long as God determines. I am here regardless of whether I am desperate, happy, distraught, or exceptionally accomplished. I am here until I have learned all the lessons necessary for my soul, completed the mission God planned for me and until His will decides it's time for me to go home.

That is who I am and why I am here.

What has bubbled up to *your* awareness?

For those of you who meditate, the practice is to ask these four questions three times: "Who am I?" "What do I want?" "What are my unique talents to share?" and "What am I grateful for?" You might prefer to ask these questions first and then work your way up to the questions I ask and the exercise I just described. Feel free to do what your heart is comfortable with.

Remember, you started reading this book because your heart yearned for the answers. Here's one way how you can receive some answers.

CHAPTER 9

Being a person of faith does not mean having an easy life. It doesn't mean having an easier life than most, either. No, not at all. Being a person of faith simply means that when you find yourself tossed overboard in a horrible storm of life, as you're flailing and gasping for air and swimming your hardest, there's a part of you that knows that the buoy has already been thrown to you. You just have to swim to where it is to find it. Sometimes, you just have to open your eyes and heart to realize the buoy is right there next to you.

Think about this for a moment. Our Blessed Virgin Mary is probably the strongest example of a faith-based human being possible. Right? As we believe and know, she was chosen by God to be the mother of our Lord. She was chosen. She was blessed. However, in spite of everything, even the Virgin Mary had to endure the worst loss a mother can experience – the death of her child! Even though chosen by God, she still had to experience the most bitter of life's experiences.

You, me, us – we regular mere mortals have to go through life. How we experience it depends on our perspective. How much faith we truly have in our hearts is what changes what we learn from these experiences. Hot air, bragging, and fake talk means nothing to God. He knows what's truly going on in our hearts. Remember, He knows what our intention is.

51

Please don't get me wrong. Even I, during tough chapters in my own life, have fallen flat on my face. Even I questioned why I was still here. Even I doubted. I'm in no way, shape, or form better than anyone else. I'm simply giving a voice to the conclusions that I've come to after so many chapters in my life. Because of my vocation as a therapist, I'm in a position where I get to help thousands of people through their individual storms. Helping clients has illuminated countless unthinkable scenarios for me, where, through prayer and being open to God's words, I have been guided to share and explain things that He has wanted me to share.

However, because of my humanity, there have also been times where my heart knew the answer, but my human brain kept questioning and torturing me. There have been times where it would have been incredibly easier for me IF I had indeed simply died.

I remember, in the beginning of the Covid-19 pandemic, I got sick. I don't usually get sick. I hadn't had a fever since I turned 10 years of age, but one day in April 2020, I woke up horribly sick. I woke up thinking the house was on fire, that's how high my fever was. I ached - everywhere. Everything within me hurt. Blinking my eyes aggravated a splitting headache that lasted for days. Yes, it truly was that bad. I could barely move. I was in that state for four days. I was too nauseous to eat, but kept sipping water so as not to become dangerously dehydrated.

During those four days, it would truly have been better for me to just die. I prayed for death. I asked to die. I begged God to take me home. I pondered what leaving this body would feel like. I prepared myself for that momentous moment when I came face to face with God, but alas my consciousness remained firmly attached to this human shell. So, there I was, in severely intense physical pain, praying, having this discussion with God about why He chose to leave me in the body. And... I got the answer, "Because you Maureen, are half-baked!"

Half-baked?!?!?! I remember jolting up, the sudden movement jarring every nerve into shocking intensities of pain, but I was stunned with the response. "Half-baked?" What could He possibly mean by that? So, I asked, and in that moment of full awareness, the answer was "You have too many experiences yet to live, so much love to experience and receive, so much success and serving yet to do......you're only half-baked! You're not done yet. You're not ready yet." And there amidst all the physical discomfort that was beyond painful, my heart and soul were soothed.

Let's bring it down to normal life again. Let's say a parent takes their child to the dentist. You would agree that this is a wise decision, fair? It's a parent's responsibility to ensure that their child's health, including their dental health, be at its best, right? So, let's say the dentist needs to fill a cavity or perform an extraction. The parent is fully aware that the injections, although painful, are necessary. Yet the parent makes the educated decision that the temporary discomfort the child is going to experience is acceptable because of the long-term health benefits their child is going to receive following the treatment. Fair?

Well, what if we had to look at God's plan for us in the same manner? Yes, I'm falling into the personification trap that I mentioned earlier. However, I ask that you give me some leeway for a few minutes. Can you see how if we as humans can understand that God has a bigger plan for us, that He has a better perspective, that what we might consider painful chapters of our lives are just *temporary discomfort* that's absolutely necessary for us to be ready - mind, brain, body, and soul - to receive the blessings that follow it?

CHAPTER 10

When someone we know dies, can we predict how we're going to react? What are we expected to do when we have to deal with the reality and practicality of life **before** we can process the fact that someone we loved dearly has died?

In regular life, we all know about the Fight/Flight response. Well, truth be told, the full set of survival mechanisms is Fight, Flight, Freeze, Food, & Fornication. Yes, all five. When we face a crisis, a horrendous situation, our consciousness falls into the Primitive Mind functioning, which is the reptilian portion of the brain. Once there, all we can handle is the most basic of living functions, and those are our survival mechanisms. Each of us is wired in a certain way. We are born with specific wiring. There is no right or wrong, they are simply different.

Let's say that you witness a horrible car crash. If you're wired with "Fight" as your survival mechanism, then you will run to the crash site to help. Your response is *action*. If you're wired with "Flight," then you will walk away from the site. Your response is to *flee*. If you're wired with "Freeze," then you will be stuck there, sometimes unable to even speak. Your response is to *stay put*. If you're wired with "Food," then you will go in search of a donut. Your response is to *eat* to ensure that you're alive tomorrow. If you're wired with "Fornication," then you will go and have sex. Your response is to *attempt to ensure your immortality by procreating*. Yes, it is that basic of a response.

55

As it is in regular life, so it is when dealing with a death. Whichever way you're wired is how you will respond. There is no right or wrong. There only is. When it comes to dealing with the death and the loss of a loved one, one can appreciate that someone has to oversee the practical goings on, right? Someone must organize the funeral and everything that goes with it, right?

So, what happens if the person in charge of handling everything is the one wired with "Fight?" In that case, there is a congruency of energy and *taking action* which helps that individual through their pain, because handling all the arrangements is in alignment with how their brain needs to function. But what if the person handling all the arrangements is wired to "Freeze?" That's where you see nervous breakdowns happen. It's not that they are incapable of handling the situation. They're unable to face them because their unconscious mind is stuck on "Freeze," which usually means the inability to choose which action to take, an inability to make a decision. However, organizing the funeral and everything else means making countless decisions. This, of course, creates extreme opposing energies within that individual, which stresses him/her out to the point of having a crisis.

What happens to the ones who are wired with "Fight" and they do take the necessary actions and handle everything? When do they get to grieve? Even the strongest of the strong at some point needs to break down and sob. Even the most stoic person at some point needs to release all the pain. If the rest of the family is wired with all the other choices, someone needs to realize that the one organizing everything also needs down time.

Dare to ask
Maureen Pisani

There's something else I need to bring up here. When one is wired with "Fornication" as a survival mechanism, one really can't help oneself. Acknowledging that one instinctively desires sex when in a crisis usually causes one to self-judge particularly harshly. However, please keep in mind, that it truly is a survival mechanism. Of course, I would advise to be prudent about what and with whom you share this information, but for the sake of self-forgiveness, please see this aspect of yourself as the most human aspect of your incredibly human Homo sapiens existence.

CHAPTER 11

As soon as a death occurs, grief follows. My definition of the progression of grief is this.

Imagine walking with a pebble in your shoe. Sometimes the pebble is beneath your heel and it hurts. Another time, the pebble is beneath your big toe, and it hurts there too. Then at a different time, the pebble is beneath your arch, and it hurts there, too. The progression of grief (how one goes through life to come to some semblance of normalcy) is when the pebble finally settles in that space between your baby toe and the shoe. It's still there. You're still aware of its presence, but you're now able to walk with the least amount of pain possible.

Grieving is an incredibly personal process. If you can remember anything from this book, please remember this. *No one can ever tell you to "get over it." No one has the right to tell you that you've grieved enough. No one can ever determine how many months or years your heart is going to require for you to come to terms with the loss.* Yes, "come to terms" with it, not accept it. When we lose a loved one, we know that the world was a better place with him/her in it. Coming to terms with the reality of the loss is simply acquiescing to the fact that the death did happen, and that somehow in spite and despite everything you've been through, you continued breathing, functioning and living.

How does one grieve? There isn't a right or wrong way to grieve. There's only your way to grieve. Sometimes grieving presents as crying inconsolably; at other times it's being quiet while remembering an endearing moment between the two of you. Sometimes, it's that thought "oh, he/she would have loved this meal," while at other times, simply watching one of his/her favorite movies helps you feel closer to them.

My Dad went "home" 18 years ago. Most days I can share a favorite memory of his with a smile and a chuckle. However, there are days, when I'm on the couch sobbing my heart out feeling like he just died yesterday. There is no right or wrong, there only **is**. The one thing I am conscious of is that when I have those teary moments, I do have them in private.

As your therapist, I can't be objective in session, where I'm pledged to being your sounding board, your voice of reason, if I'm sobbing with you. I can share with you, for authenticity's sake that I understand your wound and pain, but I have to keep it together. You deserve my best.

When one researches grief, of course one will find the Kubler-Ross standard "5 stages of grief:" Loss/Denial, Anger, Depression, Bargaining, and Acceptance. No one goes through these stages linearly. You won't spend one month in each stage and then magically switch over the next, and the next. No, in actuality, we go through these stages of grief like a ball in a pinball machine. We bounce off each and land with a hard thud onto one or the other, without rhyme or reason.

You can be in complete denial at 10 a.m. and then find yourself bargaining with God, offering your best behavior in exchange for one more hug from that person at 2 p.m., and then feeling completely depressed, deflated, sad, and empty by 6 p.m. Another distinction that I do need to clarify is that "acceptance" does not mean "I'm okay with the fact that '_____' died." No.

All it means is that at some point in time, your mind goes from thinking of that person and having a saber go through your heart yet again, to simply acknowledging that this is how life will be from here on out.

One thing that truly makes a difference is having someone who can really listen to you. Yes, I am here for you. Yes, a therapist can definitely help, but if that's not an option, find a grief counselor, a priest, a spiritual confidant, or basically, a person who understands what maintaining confidentiality truly is. During the grieving process, our minds, both conscious and unconscious, are scrambling for answers they can't find, recognize, or accept. Our hearts are shattered. What used to be our life is unrecognizable. What used to be our future is now completely foreign to us. What we thought was solid has disintegrated. What we could visualize has disappeared, and what we thought made sense has become illogical.

When we're going through such a loss, words come out, words we don't mean, words we would never consider or think of saying otherwise. But these words do escape our lips, and so we need to be around someone who is simply holding space for us. Holding space with a non-judgmental attitude, with *quiet acceptance of us,* as their answer to all our questions.

Dare to ask
Maureen Pisani

When we're going through such a tragedy, we ask questions. Hundreds, thousands of questions. Some questions, no one has the answers to. Sometimes, all our heart requires is that we ask the question. Sometimes, we are not looking for an answer. Sometimes, simply stating it out loud relieves the pressure, eases the pain, and soothes our soul. All the other person has to do is be there, present, attentive, truly listening to us.

When does one grieve? Ironically, regardless of personality, which only determines whether one grieves in public (extrovert) or in private (introvert), we grieve when either the pain is just too much to bear, or when our heart feels ready to face another iota of acknowledgement of the loss.

There is something I need to add here. Technically speaking, when we lose someone we love dearly, the grieving never ends. All that we do is get accustomed to every day being just a little less bright, a little more stark, a little off. Because the truth of the matter is, that after experiencing a loss of that magnitude, life will never go back to normal.

That's where a lot of people get confused. There's this false expectation that at some point, life will get back to normal, but how can it? Normal means with that person in it, but that person has died, so returning to that prior "setting" of life is impossible to achieve. Life will go back to being mundane, back to being practical, back to being filled with the minutia of life that keeps the world spinning, businesses running, and families living... but never back to what used to be.

I recommend allowing life to recalibrate in a way where obvious adjustments are made, where apart from being practical and grounded, one is also simply open to seeing how this new version of life is going to come to fruition.

The first year is the hardest of them all. Each of us goes through "oh this is the first _____ that he/she is not here," regardless of whether it is their anniversary or our own special day. It's a normal human experience to honor, notate, or even call loved ones to share that "today" is *this* day for you.

Of course, as the years go by, especially during the holidays, that person will be mentioned. Their favorite dish will be dedicated to them. Their quirky silly jokes will be recounted, but there won't be an empty seat at the table any longer. There will be an acknowledgment of the loss, which will be balanced with the practicality of having a full table filled with joy and love.

CHAPTER 12

So, when does one stop grieving? How is one supposed to move on to their normal life?

Truth be told, after losing a loved one, we just get used to living life at 99%, because it will never be 100% again. We always go back to that part of us that still grieves. There is nothing wrong with knowing and acknowledging that.

When people reach the point where life is almost back to normal, and they've reached the 99% mark, it might also feel to them like they've stopped loving their deceased loved one. That's never the case. Some people get stuck in the depths of despair because they think the more *they* suffer, the more that translates to how much they loved the deceased. It doesn't. Suffering and loving aren't dependent on each other.

There are others who think that if they return to functioning fully in their life, then that means they've forgotten the deceased loved one. They punish themselves for the fleeting moments of joy or laughter that they experience. This is also incorrect.

Your loved ones love you. They wish for you to be happy. There is absolutely nothing wrong with you laughing out loud because a joke was funny. There is absolutely nothing wrong with you feeling great about how your business is growing, or how much you enjoyed your dinner. There is nothing wrong about singing your favorite song. However, some refrain from doing these, because they feel that they are somehow not honoring their loved one's memory.

Every year, the anniversary day of my Dad's death used to be a day where I hid and mourned him. This year, thanks to a close friend who has a deep understanding of life, death, and faith, we transformed that energy completely. This year, I honored my Dad by preparing all his favorite foods and celebrated his incredible taste and palate, with one of the most decadent meals ever. Ever dish came with a story. Every story led to me sharing something touching, loving, funny, and adorable about my Dad. To my surprise, that day turned out to be a happy day, overflowing with great memories and love. Now, I know that if asked, my Dad would share that he too preferred the way I chose to celebrate him this year versus all the other years.

There is something you too can do to keep your loved ones "alive." When appropriate, share a story, an anecdote, or an idiosyncrasy about them. This has incredible benefits. It will lift your heart up, it will keep them in your day-to-day existence, it will help someone else see things differently, and it will make your loved one incredibly happy to see you smiling.

CHAPTER 13

As we go through this journey of exploration and discussion, it's now time to discuss another sensitive and controversial topic: the soul. Specifically, what happens to the soul after we die?

According to some schools of thought, as soon as the soul leaves the body, it is instantly face to face with God where it is judged. We are also taught that if the soul is deemed to go to heaven, after the soul is cleansed in purgatory, then it will get to enjoy being in God's Eternal and Unconditional love for Eternity. However, if the soul is sent to hell, then it is sent to a space which is void of God's love.

We have also been taught that Heaven is "above" while Hell is "below." However, we know that location is also a human concept. Considering that heaven is a space that's filled with God's love and hell is a space that is empty of God's love, does there really need to be a location?

What if the souls aren't "above" or "beneath" us? What if all the souls are just in a different realm, one most human physical bodies and brains cannot perceive? What if the souls are all around us? How many times have you seen something out of the corner of your eye, only to look at what caught your attention and see nothing? How many times have you had that sensation that "___" was around you? How many times did you feel his/her presence? How many of you *saw* your loved one for a split second, for a blink of an eye, to then dismiss it as your eyes playing tricks on you?

How many times did you smell his cologne or her perfume, only to shrug it off as a silly coincidence? What if it were real? Well, what would happen if that were true?

Yes, there's a definite reason I'm sharing this. In my opinion, once a loved one releases their physical body, their soul is pure energy – this amazing consciousness that is fully aware. This consciousness is who they were, the part of them that lived and loved and is still 100% alive! The only difference is that they are no longer tethered to the physical realm. They have access to every plane and every energy.

There are some of you who are going to adamantly disagree with me on this. That is more than understandable to me. I would like you to pause for a second to remind you of the Iceberg-Congo-tribe scenario. I totally understand that just because some of you haven't experienced these topics, it simply means that you haven't experienced them, not that those experiences aren't true. And there are some of you who are wondering if you can risk opening up to the possibility of believing me. Because I know for a fact that there are some of you who also know that what I'm sharing is the absolute truth.

Some have asked why they never experience any of these situations. I ask them if they believe that visitations from their loved ones are possible. They adamantly negate that it's even possible. So, is it so surprising that their loved ones do not visit them? If one is sending out the energetic message that connection is impossible, can you really blame the deceased loved ones for not reaching out?

As soon as we start going down the "soul" and "soul interaction" topics, we open the discussion to what the public calls *ghosts.* I find it incredibly interesting when some out there will, with full force, state "ghosts do not exist." Oh really? I will urge you to circle back to that question – Do you believe that God is omnipotent? Because if you do, you know that God can create everything and anything – including ghosts.

So, let's go down this rabbit hole, shall we? What exactly are ghosts? The definition of a ghost is *an apparition of a dead person which is believed to appear or become manifest to the living, typically as a nebulous image.* Basically, it's the soul, what we established as his/her life essence, showing up in a manner where it can be perceived through our human physical senses.

I need to explain something extremely important. [For those of you who might be coming to some premature conclusions, please keep in mind that NEVER have I EVER played with anything occult. Until this very moment, I have never even touched the box of a Ouija board, let alone interacted with the board itself (and never will).] When I share an experience I had, it's because it happened spontaneously, and I reacted instinctively. In my world, because I didn't go and *test things out* or *provoke situations,* yet these events still occurred, then in my opinion, they were meant to happen to me. I was meant to notice and experience them. Those events were meant for me.

If my Dad wishes to visit me, he does. The easiest way to explain my experiences with my Dad is that I am aware of his presence, because he's my Daddy. I know he loves me. I also know that the love we share is eternal and unbreakable. There is nothing to fear. When he visits me, it's joy that I experience, not shock or fright.

I know of cases where people have seen their loved one in full Technicolor, as solid as you or I, where the visit lasted a few moments enough to imprint of their hearts that the deceased was more than okay. Others have heard their names being called by the deceased loved ones. Others had radios play the loved one's favorite songs, while others had electronic equipment go wonky when the loved one's energy was present.

I know of a case where a lady's loved one visited her, did what he did normally, including kissing his wife goodnight, and she freaked out! She was in hysterics! I appreciate the notion that when one comes from the world where these interactions are impossible, to live them can be jarring, but this was her loving husband of many decades. He had crossed time and space to show her how much he still loved her, and her response was screaming and crying for hours on end. Yes, he never visited her again. I guess it was too traumatizing for both of them.

I had a client whose wife "communicated" through a particular lamp. It was her favorite lamp in the house. After her passing, she would make it flicker to let her husband know she was around. It became this incredible thread of connectivity between them. Although initially skeptical, he started asking questions and deciphered a code for "yes" and for "no," and through this system and was able to get answers directly from his wife from the other side.

Years ago, when I was married, one particular floorboard in the hallway would squeak nonstop during the night. This floorboard was incredibly unique. One had to step on the northwest corner and only on the northwest corner for it to squeak. And it did – incessantly, night after night, when technically, everyone was asleep.

One night, I was exhausted, and this squeaking was driving me crazy, so I sat up in bed and out loud said "Listen, I need to sleep. I have a big day tomorrow, so can you please stop that?" And it did. It stopped. There wasn't a peep – nothing. The then-husband was taken aback by my behavior and its results, and was beyond weirded out.

I know of a case where this lady was living in an apartment where a lot of inexplicable sounds would occur. Pots and pans would clink, cupboard doors would slam, and shower doors would rattle. It was obvious to her that *somebody* wanted to make sure she knew they were there.

One evening, after returning home from work, while removing the Tupperware container from the plastic bag it was in, she noticed that the bag had moved. On a hunch, she took the opportunity and said out loud "I know you think you live here, but right now I'm living here too. I'm going to offer you a deal, ok? While it's just me alone, between 6 a.m. and 11:30 p.m. do whatever you want. Okay? However, if I have friends over, and between 11:30 p.m. and 6 a.m. you must be quiet. Okay? If you agree, push the bag." And the bag was pushed down! She remembered staring at the bag – shocked, in awe, surprised and flabbergasted all at the same time! And yes, that agreement was maintained for the duration of her living there.

I know of a case where a young woman would be awakened in the middle of the night with the sensation that someone was staring at her. Well, one night she woke up and found out who it was. He was of medium height, chubby, with long curly blonde hair, with a scruffy beard. There he was, leaning against the closet door, with his arms crossed staring at her. She could see him in enough detail, but he still looked a little transparent. Sometimes, their humanness comes through. Apparently, he must have lived there, so it would make sense that he'd be curious as to who exactly she was and what exactly she was doing in *his* apartment!

Sometimes, ghosts visit to soothe our souls, while sometimes they're attached to the building because something happened there and they're not sure how to get out of it or where to go from there. Sometimes, the death happens so fast that they don't realize they're dead. So, they linger there, unsure as to why everybody else doesn't recognize or acknowledge their presence.

Dare to ask
Maureen Pisani

There are some schools of thought that believe that each of us is walking around with our own entourage. This is where our family, immediate family, grandparents, great aunts and uncles, even ancestors surround us, to shower us with blessings and love, to guide us, to protect us and to welcome us home, when our time on earth is up.

Interactions with our loved ones do not have to be only with their spirits, though. They send us countless messages, clues, and signs. How many of you have an association with a special loved one? Some of you know your loved one is around when a dragonfly crosses your path, while others connect with the love they shared with their loved one when butterflies are around. Others hear wind chimes. There could be something incredibly specific that the loved one sends as a message that will instantly let you know that it's him/her.

I know of a case where a lady's late husband would infuse the air around her with the scent of his beard dye! It was something that was unique to him. He would do this regularly while she was driving alone in her car. For her, it meant that he was with her and that soothed her soul and diminished the pain of his loss.

In another case, this woman's godfather would introduce his presence as the unique smell that the client associated with her godfather's kitchen! There was a particular smell that his kitchen had, so if she became aware of that scent, to her it meant that he was there.

Unfortunately, sometimes, they also share what they felt as their exiting emotions. I know of a case where a man, upon walking into the location where his wife had passed, felt intense anxiety like he had never experienced before. As he walked through the location, the anxiety intensified to desperation, and built up to a paralyzing fear where his entire body was shaking. It was so intense that he had to be helped out of the building! Upon exiting the building, all the emotions and sensations slowly diminished and eventually subsided. He was shaken up because he realized that as she had dropped to the ground with a massive heart attack, his wife had been aware of what was happening and had gone through all those emotions before dying.

Here's something my Dad does with me. My Dad died on July 25th. He sends me his "725" whenever there's an important event in my life and he wants me to know that he's giving his approval. His "thumbs up," so to speak. When I attended hypnotherapy college, I started in June, and being that it was a 12-month program, it ended in June. However, my diploma and my Director's Award have July 25th as the date of graduation. Now, think about it for a second. If it was a simple mistake from the college, wouldn't it have been July 23rd, or July 28th? But no, because it was Dad letting me know that he approved and gave his blessings in this next chapter of my life – the dates on the diploma and on the marble plaque are July 25th!

I remember how nervous and rushed I was the day I was driving to give my first presentation at UCLA. I wanted to be early, and as soon as I got on the 405 freeway, it was packed. It was what the Angelinos call a "parking lot!" There I was, fretting, sweating bullets because there was no way I could be late... when all of a sudden there it was! A license plate that instead of the usual number/letter configuration had "CARMELO" on it! Yes, this license plate had my Dad's full name on it! As soon as I saw that, this eerie, yet welcome calmness washed over me. I instantly knew that I'd be there early, and everything would go smoothly. And it did! That was my Dad's way of showing me he was with me!

There are other situations where the ground itself has the connection to the "other side," and whatever is built on it will then trigger the activity. Even though some people who live there might not believe, the location itself will be active even when the residents are in complete denial.

I know of a case where this apartment complex had a tremendous amount of activity. One person was aware that things were happening, but others weren't of the same frame of mind. Then something happened that was undeniable. The woman who lived in that apartment was out of town, but her neighbors reported hearing blood-curdling screams coming from inside her apartment, to the point where they convinced the landlord to open the apartment and check.

Upon entering the apartment, the landlord and the neighbors saw that everything was in place and nobody was there, but the screaming had been undeniable. It was later discovered that that apartment building had been built on a Native American burial ground. Now, that makes that blood-curdling scream totally understandable, doesn't it?

There are some of you who are beyond sensitive to these phenomena. There are others who are completely oblivious to all these energies and souls. Neither is right or wrong. One is or isn't. It's just as simple as that. If one is aware of all the energies around, that doesn't make them good or bad, that just makes them aware. If someone else is totally unaware, so be it. The clash happens if one decides to judge the other about being right or wrong.

I know some of you are thinking that this is all baloney, but I also know that some are realizing that everything they've experienced and haven't shared with anyone, actually *did* happen.

The best way I have found to explain why *sensitive* people experience so much is this way: imagine you're in a plane, you know how we can see the upper layer of clouds? Well, for the souls floating around, let's say the world looks like a layer of clouds. The sensitive people stick out of that layer like lighthouses.

Sensitives have this energetic beacon that the souls who are lost, confused, stuck, searching for someone or something, are attracted to. These souls are attracted to the sensitive's energy because at the very least they are in desperate need of recognition. If the sensitive isn't aware that they are sensitive, they'll chalk it all up to weird coincidences. However, if the sensitive is aware, then they know to acknowledge the soul and send it to the white light.

There are some whose need for answers propels them to work with mediums. The disclaimer that I always include is that yes, some are quacks, but there are also some who are the real deal. If you're ever curious as to whom to work with, reach out to me. I will introduce you to mediums and medicine men & women who are the real deal.

However, if you're experiencing situations in your living space, and you'd like to test things out and find out for yourself who is in your space, here's an exercise you can do that will give you results in a way that will satisfy even your own skeptic mind.

In a room where there is no cross current or AC draft, tape a white piece of paper to a surface. Once it's taped, prepare a few cards, I use 3x5 cards cut in half, with questions written on them in a yes or no format. For example, "Are you my _____?" or "Are you feeling better?" or "Is grandma with you?" or "Are you moving things around?" or "Are you _____ (with a name) moving things around?" - those kinds of questions.

Once you have all the questions written, place the cards on the white paper and while holding the card steady, trace an outline around them. Once you have all the cards outlined, and when you're sure you don't need to touch them again, say out loud, "To whomever is here with me, I have set out some questions for you. Please move the cards that have a "Yes" answer." Then walk away. Leave everything there. Don't touch them. Don't check on them for at least a couple of days. If there are "Yes" answers, those cards will be moved. If after 3-5 days, none of the cards have been moved, then that means they are all "No" answers. If you need further clarification, ask different questions. I've had several clients do this exercise only to receive incredible responses.

When this line of communication is achieved, there is no loss, no disconnect, because now you have found a way to connect with your loved ones in real time.

If you're aware that there are energies around you, but you're not sure what to do, here's something that will help you determine if the energy is positive or negative.

Allow your mind to direct you to where you feel the energy is and think/say "I love you." If it's a positive energy, it will accept the love and stay. If it's a negative energy, because love is the emotion it detests the most, it will instantly leave your space.

Here's something I composed that helps me to filter out negative energies and allows positive energies to stay (IF that is what you desire).

The Invitation

For whomever is here right now...
If you are an angel, an archangel, a guide, a loved one, or
you're coming from the
White light to help me, you may stay.
Do not disturb me, let me be.
Do not interrupt my sleep, let me sleep all night through.

However, if you are from the dark light,
YOU ARE FORBIDDEN!
You are to leave my space, my house, my energy right now!
Be gone now and forever!

Archangels, guardian angels and loved ones,
protect me, protect my family
and
protect my home.

Thank you. Thank you. Thank you.

If you have an experience that leaves you slightly rattled, here's something that works wonders in getting one to feel safe and protected.

Dare to ask
Maureen Pisani

Think of the Archangels, especially Michael, who is known as "The Protector." They have been depicted to be at least 7 feet tall. Imagine Archangel Michael standing in front of you. Visualize him leaning in to hug you, but it's not just a simple hug. As Archangel Michael is hugging you, he also wraps his wings around you. Visualize being cocooned inside his arms and wings where you are beyond safe, protected, and loved. Remember that angels are messengers of God and are also pure love. Once ensconced in his wings, all you have to do is simply receive all of his and God's blessings.

CONCLUSION

If you asked 6 of your friends to make spaghetti their way and then bring it over, you'd have 6 versions of spaghetti, right? Because each of them learned it differently, each of them has different traditions, slightly different recipes, and slightly different preferences, right? So, if there all these different versions about something as simple as spaghetti, can you see how natural it is for us to have different versions and opinions about death, dying, and what happens after death?

Now because I am me, I can share with you how I've experienced the loss of loved ones, the process of people dying, and what I've been taught happens afterward. So, it's more than fair that you experience it your way.

However, if you're at a point where you're not quite sure, please feel free to borrow my thinking, my rationalizations, my experiences, and my conclusions. It'll make my day to know that my sharing my outlook on these topics has helped you.

You don't have to believe me. Do the research for yourself. Find scholars, mystics, or authentic spiritual or religious leaders. Find whomever your heart resonates with and ask. We are dealing with a topic that opens the metaphysical and the mystical worlds to us.

It is more than understandable to have differing opinions. My intention for this book is to offer different perspectives, to get one to be open to possibilities, and to offer different schools of thought that ease the grief.

Dare to ask
Maureen Pisani

If reading this book launches you into a spiritual journey, then it has served its purpose.

If you still have questions, please feel free to reach out to me. It will be my honor to be of service.

The one thing I will leave you with is something I truly believe. Everything happens for a reason, and that reason is there to serve you. Do your best to live life from a perspective of love. That's the one currency that every heart can recognize and receive.

We know that *God is Love* and after all is said and done, aren't we all created in God's image?

BIOGRAPHY

Maureen Pisani is a Certified Master Hypnotherapist and the founder of Pro Thrive Science Based Hypnotherapy, where she works with individuals and groups (both in-person and online) to help empower, streamline success, and truly thrive. Maureen is also a world-renowned Motivational Speaker and was the Resident Hypnotherapist at the Chopra Center (Carlsbad, CA) until its closure in December 2019.

Aside from being a Hypnotherapist, she is also a Master Practitioner of Emotional Freedom Technique (EFT Tapping), Therapeutic Guided Imagery, and Reiki Energy work. Maureen is also a Trainer in Neuro-Linguistic Programming (NLP). She employs a variety of modalities when working with her clients to bring them the best tools and resources for positive and lasting change. Maureen has also been a Director, Instructor, and Mentor at two nationally accredited universities, where she shared her love and knowledge of Hypnotherapy with her many students.

As of December 2020, she has published 16 books and has co-authored a research paper issued by the Neuroscience Department at UCLA.

Maureen Pisani is the poster child for how hypnotherapy can help change your life for the better. After an accident left her in constant pain, she found Hypnotherapy, which offered her relief and a new lease on life. She went from being 100% disabled to being in the top 1% of her profession.

Although she now lives in San Diego, CA, Maureen is originally from the Island of Malta, and continues to share her love of her home country with all those she encounters. In her free time, she enjoys dancing, knitting blankets for premature babies, and gardening. If you're interested in Hypnotherapy, please contact Maureen at www.ProThriveSBH.com. She'll be happy to answer your questions.

Other books by author

- **Against All Odds**
- **Invisible to Invincible**
- **'Timeless Hypnotic Scripts I'**
- **'Timeless Hypnotic Scripts II'**
- **21 Days to Launch 2021**
  - Hypnotherapy & EFT Workbook with 1 Hypnotic MP3
- **Conquering Covid-19 (Also titled as "Conquering Crisis")**
  - Hypnotherapy & EFT Workbook with 1 Hypnotic MP3
- **3 Easy Steps to achieve *SUCCESS***
  - Hypnotherapy & EFT Workbook with 3 Hypnotic MP3s
- **3 Easy Steps for *Relationships***
  - Hypnotherapy & EFT Workbook with 3 Hypnotic MP3s
- **3 Easy Steps for *Weight Management***
  - Hypnotherapy & EFT Workbook with 3 Hypnotic MP3s
- **3 Easy Steps for a successful '*Hypnotherapy Practice*'**
  - Hypnotherapy & EFT Workbook with 3 Hypnotic MP3s

83

- **3 Easy Steps for *Resilience***
  - ○ Hypnotherapy & EFT Workbook with 1 Hypnotic MP3

- **Living a Pain & Medication Free Life**
  - ○ Hypnotherapy & EFT Workbook with 1 Hypnotic MP3
- **R.I.D. Relieving Intestinal Discomfort**
  - ○ Hypnotherapy & EFT Workbook with 1 Hypnotic MP3
- **'401 Study Guide'**
  - ○ Supplementary Textbook to HMI 401 Course
- **Getting Away with it**
  - ○ A fictional romance

Dare to ask
Maureen Pisani

Made in the USA
Middletown, DE
01 May 2021